The Hagopian Institute, LLC has compiled the _Quote Junkie_ series. The overall series includes over 8,000 quotes, focusing mostly on short quotes that can be used in everyday life as sources of wisdom and inspiration. This particular edition of the series includes quotes about business, and quotes that can be used in business settings to motivate yourself and your employees. Please enjoy, and share these quotes with your co-workers, friends and family.

Todd Hagopian

President

The Hagopian Institute, LLC

I0455518

The rule of my life is to make business a pleasure, and pleasure my business.

Aaron Burr

Everybody likes a compliment.

Abraham Lincoln

Books serve to show a man that those original thoughts of his aren't very new at all.

Abraham Lincoln

Give me six hours to chop down a tree and I will spend the first four sharpening the axe.

Abraham Lincoln

I will prepare and some day my chance will come.

Abraham Lincoln

Some single mind must be master, else there will be no agreement in anything.

Abraham Lincoln

Things may come to those who wait, but only the things left by those who hustle.

Abraham Lincoln

When I do good, I feel good. When I do bad, I feel bad. That's my religion.

Abraham Lincoln

Am I not destroying my enemies when I make friends of them?

Abraham Lincoln

Don't worry when you are not recognized, but strive to be worthy of recognition

Abraham Lincoln

I never had a policy; I have just tried to do my very best each and every day.

Abraham Lincoln

I walk slowly, but I never walk backward.

Abraham Lincoln

My great concern is not whether you have failed, but whether you are content with your failure.

Abraham Lincoln

Adventure upon all the tickets in the lottery, and you lose for certain; and the greater the number of your tickets the nearer your approach to this certainty.

Adam Smith

What we have done for ourselves alone dies with us; what we have done for others and the world remains and is immortal.

Albert Pike

Instinct is untaught ability.

Alexander Bain

There is nothing impossible to him who will try.

Alexander The Great

My view is different. Public relations are a key component of any operation in this day of instant communications and rightly inquisitive citizens.

Alvin Adams

It is always the simple that produces the marvelous.

Amelia Barr

Don't be content with doing only your duty. Do more than your duty. It's the horse that finishes a neck ahead wins the race.

Andrew Carnegie

The average person puts only 25% of his energy and ability into his work. The world takes off its hat to those who put in more than 50% of their capacity, and stands on its head for those few and far between souls who devote 100%.

Andrew Carnegie

There is little success where there is little laughter.

Andrew Carnegie

Teamwork is the ability to work together toward a common vision. It is the fuel that allows common people to attain uncommon results.

Andrew Carnegie

Surplus wealth is a sacred trust which its possessor is bound to administer in his lifetime for the good of the community.

Andrew Carnegie

The secret of success lies not in doing your own work, but in recognizing the right man to do it.

Andrew Carnegie

As I grow older, I pay less attention to what men say. I just watch what they do.

Andrew Carnegie

Concentration is my motto - first honesty, then industry, then concentration.

Andrew Carnegie

I shall argue that strong men, conversely, know when to compromise and that all principles can be compromised to serve a greater principle

Andrew Carnegie

The first man gets the oyster, the second man gets the shell.

Andrew Carnegie

The men who have succeeded are men who have chosen one line and stuck to it.

Andrew Carnegie

If I am shot at, I want no man to be in the way of the bullet.

Andrew Johnson

He who is to be a good ruler must have first been ruled.

Aristotle

No excellent soul is exempt from a mixture of madness.

Aristotle

The whole is more than the sum of its parts.

Aristotle

Men acquire a particular quality by constantly acting in a particular way.

Aristotle

No one loves the man whom he fears.

Aristotle

Pleasure in the job puts perfection in the work.

Aristotle

Well begun is half done.

Aristotle

What it lies in our power to do, it lies in our power not to do.

Aristotle

In a balanced organization, working towards a common objective, there is success.

Arthur Helps

Routine is not organization, any more than paralysis is order.

Arthur Helps

Wealth is like sea-water; the more we drink, the thirstier we become; and the same is true of fame.

Arthur Shopenhauer

Talent hits a target no one else can hit; Genius hits a target no one else can see.

Arthur Shopenhauer

It is a clear gain to sacrifice pleasure in order to avoid pain.

Arthur Shopenhauer

A single lie destroys a whole reputation of integrity.

Baltasar Gracian

Let the first impulse pass, wait for the second.

Baltasar Gracian

Never open the door to the lesser evil, for other and greater ones invariably slink in after it.

Baltasar Gracian

A wise man gets more use from his enemies than a fool from his friends.

Baltasar Gracian

Advice is sometimes transmitted more successfully through a joke than grave teaching.

Baltasar Gracian

Don't take the wrong side of an argument just because your opponent has taken the right side.

Baltasar Gracian

It is better to sleep on things beforehand than lie awake about them afterwards.

Baltasar Gracian

It is good to vary in order that you may frustrate the curious, especially those who envy you.

Baltasar Gracian

Never have a companion that casts you in the shade.

Baltasar Gracian

Quit while you're ahead. All the best gamblers do.

Baltasar Gracian

We often have to put up with most from those on whom we most depend.

Baltasar Gracian

Without courage, wisdom bears no fruit.

Baltasar Gracian

Work is the price which is paid for reputation.

Baltasar Gracian

I have never known any distress that an hour's reading did not relieve.

Baron de Montesquieu

In most things success depends on knowing how long it takes to succeed.

Baron de Montesquieu

To become truly great, one has to stand with people, not above them.

Baron de Montesquieu

Through perseverance many people win success out of what seemed destined to be certain failure

Benjamin Disraeli

The secret of success is constancy to purpose

Benjamin Disraeli

Ignorance never settles a question.

Benjamin Disraeli

Desperation is sometimes as powerful an inspirer as genius.

Benjamin Disraeli

Next to knowing when to seize an opportunity, the most important thing in life is to know when to forego an advantage.

Benjamin Disraeli

As a general rule the most successful man in life is the man who has the best information.

Benjamin Disraeli

Every production of genius must be the production of enthusiasm.

Benjamin Disraeli

One secret of success in life is for a man to be ready for his opportunity when it comes.

Benjamin Disraeli

Tell me and I forget. Teach me and I remember. Involve me and I learn.

Benjamin Franklin

Whatever is begun in anger ends in shame.

Benjamin Franklin

The worst wheel of the cart makes the most noise.

Benjamin Franklin

Never leave that till tomorrow which you can do today.

Benjamin Franklin

He that rises late must trot all day.

Benjamin Franklin

Either write something worth reading or do something worth writing.

Benjamin Franklin

Beware of little expenses. A small leak will sink a great ship.

Benjamin Franklin

A penny saved is a penny earned.

Benjamin Franklin

You may delay, but time will not.

Benjamin Franklin

Time is money.

Benjamin Franklin

The use of money is all the advantage there is in having it.

Benjamin Franklin

Necessity never made a good bargain.

Benjamin Franklin

It is easier to prevent bad habits than to break them.

Benjamin Franklin

He that speaks much, is much mistaken.

Benjamin Franklin

By failing to prepare, you are preparing to fail.

Benjamin Franklin

Well done is better than well said.

Benjamin Franklin

He that is good for making excuses is seldom good for anything else.

Benjamin Franklin

Never leave that till tomorrow which you can do today.

Benjamin Franklin

An investment in knowledge always pays the best interest.

Benjamin Franklin

Never confuse motion with action.

Benjamin Franklin

Do not fear mistakes. You will know failure. Continue to reach out.

Benjamin Franklin

It is easier to prevent bad habits than to break them.

Benjamin Franklin

Energy and persistence conquer all things.

Benjamin Franklin

If you would persuade, you must appeal to interest rather than intellect.

Benjamin Franklin

Drive thy business or it will drive thee.

Benjamin Franklin

He that rises late must trot all day.

Benjamin Franklin

If passion drives you, let reason hold the reins.

Benjamin Franklin

The longest sword, the strongest lungs, the most voices, are false measures of truth.

Benjamin Whichcote

Defeat should never be a source of discouragement, but rather a fresh stimulus.

Bishop Robert Smith

The way to have power is to take it.

Boss Tweed

Never let a day pass that you will have cause to say, I will do better tomorrow.

Brigham Young

Your work is to discover your work and then with all your heart to give yourself to it.

Buddha

All that we are is the result of what we have thought. The mind is everything.
What we think we become.

Buddha

He is able who thinks he is able.

Buddha

There are only two mistakes one can make along the road to truth; not going all
the way, and not starting.

Buddha

An idea that is developed and put into action is more important than an idea that
exists only as an idea.

Buddha

Chaos is inherent in all compounded things. Strive on with diligence.

Buddha

Dog is not considered a good dog because he is a good barker. A man is not
considered a good man because he is a good talker.

Buddha

I do not believe in a fate that falls on men however they act; but I do believe in a fate that falls on them unless they act.

Buddha

Don't expect to build up the weak by pulling down the strong.

Calvin Coolidge

Industry, thrift and self-control are not sought because they create wealth, but because they create character.

Calvin Coolidge

It takes a great man to be a good listener.

Calvin Coolidge

Little progress can be made by merely attempting to repress what is evil. Our great hope lies in developing what is good.

Calvin Coolidge

We cannot do everything at once, but we can do something at once.

Calvin Coolidge

No enterprise can exist for itself alone. It ministers to some great need, it performs some great service, not for itself, but for others; or failing therein, it ceases to be profitable and ceases to exist.

Calvin Coolidge

No man ever listened himself out of a job.

Calvin Coolidge

Economy is the method by which we prepare today to afford the improvements of tomorrow.

Calvin Coolidge

I praise loudly. I blame softly.

Catherine The Great

You will never find time for anything. If you want time you must make it.

Charles Bruxton

The first rule of business is: Do other men for they would do you.

Charles Dickens

The one great principle of English law is to make business for itself.

Charles Dickens

Life should not be estimated exclusively by the standard of dollars and cents.

Charles Goodyear

Look twice before you leap.

Charlotte Bronte

I am tired of talk that comes to nothing.

Chief Joseph

If a man takes no thought about what is distant, he will find sorrow near at hand.

Confucius

It does not matter how slowly you go so long as you do not stop.

Confucius

You cannot open a book without learning something.

Confucius

A superior man is modest in his speech, but exceeds in his actions.

Confucius

Do not impose on others what you yourself do not desire.

Confucius

I hear and I forget. I see and I remember. I do and I understand.

Confucius

Life is really simple, but we insist on making it complicated.

Confucius

Never contract friendship with a man that is not better than thyself.

Confucius

Only the wisest and stupidest of men never change.

Confucius

The superior man acts before he speaks, and afterwards speaks according to his action.

Confucius

When anger rises, think of the consequences.

Confucius

He who will not economize will have to agonize.

Confucius

Ability will never catch up with the demand for it.

Confucius

When you are laboring for others let it be with the same zeal as if it were for yourself.

Confucius

I don't care half so much about making money as I do about making my point, and coming out ahead.

Cornelius Vanderbilt

You have undertaken to cheat me. I won't sue you, for the law is too slow. I will ruin you.

Cornelius Vanderbilt

Our opportunities to do good are our talents

Cotton Mather

Everything in the world is purchased by labor.

David Hume

And what is the greatest number? Number one.

David Hume

Gold, on the contrary, though of little use compared with air or water, will exchange for a great quantity of other goods.

David Ricardo

There can be no rise in the value of labour without a fall of profits.

David Ricardo

It is better to destroy one's own errors than those of others.

Democritus

It is greed to do all the talking but not to want to listen at all.

Democritus

Our sins are more easily remembered than our good deeds.

Democritus

Concealed talent brings no reputation.

Desiderius Erasmus

Don't give your advice before you are called upon.

Desiderius Erasmus

Prevention is better than cure.

Desiderius Erasmus

A good portion of speaking will consist in knowing how to lie.

Desiderius Erasmus

It is astonishing what a lot of odd minutes one can catch during the day, if one really sets about it.

Dinah Maria Mulock

We have two ears and one tongue so that we would listen more and talk less.

Diogenes

Wise kings generally have wise counselors; and he must be a wise man himself who is capable of distinguishing one.

Diogenes

It takes a wise man to discover a wise man.

Diogenes

Things are worth what they will fetch at a sale

Edward Coke

Our work is the presentation of our capabilities.

Edward Gibbon

Every man should make up his own mind that if he expect to succeed, he must give an honest return for the other man's dollar.

Edward Harriman

Much good work is lost for the lack of a little more.

Edward Harriman

The greatest mistake you can make in life is continually fearing that you'll make one.

Elbert Hubbard

A man is not paid for having a head and hands, but for using them.

Elbert Hubbard

Get happiness out of your work or you may never know what happiness is.

Elbert Hubbard

Folks who never do any more than they are paid for, never get paid more than they do.

Elbert Hubbard

Know what you want to do, hold the thought firmly, and do every day what should be done, and every sunset will see you that much nearer to your goal.

Elbert Hubbard

The best preparation for good work tomorrow is to do good work today.

Elbert Hubbard

We work to become, not to acquire.

Elbert Hubbard

One machine can do the work of fifty ordinary men. No machine can do the work of one extraordinary man.

Elbert Hubbard

Pray that success will not come any faster than you are able to endure it.

Elbert Hubbard

The world is moving so fast these days that the man who says it can't be done is generally interrupted by someone doing it.

Elbert Hubbard

Measure not the work until the day's out and the labor done.

Elizabeth Barrett Browning

The cloud never comes from the quarter of the horizon from which we watch for it.

Elizabeth Gaskell

If I could I would always work in silence and obscurity, and let my efforts be known by their results.

Emily Bronte

A person who has not done one half his day's work by ten o clock, runs a chance of leaving the other half undone.

Emily Bronte

If evil be spoken of you and it be true, correct yourself, if it be a lie, laugh at it.

Epictetus

It's not what happens to you, but how you react to it that matters.

Epictetus

Know, first, who you are, and then adorn yourself accordingly.

Epictetus

Men are disturbed not by things, but by the view which they take of them.

Epictetus

No great thing is created suddenly.

Epictetus

Difficulties are things that show a person what they are.

Epictetus

If you want to improve, be content to be thought foolish and stupid.

Epictetus

One that desires to excel should endeavor in those things that are in themselves most excellent.

Epictetus

The world turns aside to let any man pass who knows where he is going.

Epictetus

Skillful pilots gain their reputation from storms and tempest.

Epictetus

The greater the difficulty, the more the glory in surmounting it.

Epictetus

Our opinions become fixed at the point where we stop thinking.

Ernest Renan

How very little can be done under the spirit of fear

Florence Nightingale

I think one's feelings waste themselves in words; they ought all to be distilled into actions which bring results.

Florence Nightingale

Affairs that depend on many rarely succeed.

Francesco Guicciardini

Many are stubborn in pursuit of the path they have chosen, few in pursuit of the goal.

Friedrich Nietzsche

The doer alone learneth.

Friedrich Nietzsche

Amid the pressure of great events, a general principle gives no help.

Georg Wilhelm Friedrich Hegel

Nothing great in the world has ever been accomplished without passion.

Georg Wilhelm Friedrich Hegel

I would be willing, yes glad, to see a battle every day during my life.

George Custer

Have the courage of your desire.

George Gissing

Money is time. With money I buy for cheerful use the hours which otherwise would not in any sense be mine; nay, which would make me their miserable bondsman.

George Gissing

Time is money says the proverb, but turn it around and you get a precious truth. Money is time.

George Gissing

The only cure for grief is action.

George Henry Lewes

To keep a lamp burning we have to keep putting oil in it.

George Macdonald

The best preparation for the future is the present well seen to, and the last duty done.

George Macdonald

To have what we want is riches; but to be able to do without is power.

George Macdonald

To be trusted is a greater complement than to be loved.

George Macdonald

Always imitate the behavior of the winners when you lose.

George Meredith

Work is not man's punishment. It is his reward and his strength and his pleasure.

George Sand

Most men make little use of their speech than to give evidence against their own understanding.

George Savile

If we are wise, let us prepare for the worst.

George Washington

Let your Discourse with Men of Business be Short and Comprehensive

George Washington

Good council has no price.

Giuseppe Mazzini

If at first you do succeed - try to hide your astonishment.

Harry Banks

Order is power.

Henri Frederic Amiel

Do not hire a man who does your work for money, but him who does it for love of it.

Henry David Thoreau

In the long run, men hit only what they aim at. Therefore, they had better aim at something high.

Henry David Thoreau

Success usually comes to those who are too busy to be looking for it.

Henry David Thoreau

If you make money your god, it will plague you like the devil.

Henry Fielding

He that respects himself is safe from others. He wears a coat of mail that none can pierce.

Henry Wadsworth Longfellow

Heights by great men reached and kept were not obtained by sudden flight but, while their companions slept, they were toiling upward in the night.

Henry Wadsworth Longfellow

Ambition is so powerful a passion in the human breast, that however high we reach we are never satisfied.

Henry Wadsworth Longfellow

It takes less time to do a thing right, than it does to explain why you did it wrong.

Henry Wadsworth Longfellow

Each morning sees some task begun, each evening sees it close; Something attempted, something done, has earned a night's repose.

Henry Wadsworth Longfellow

I never knew an early-rising, hard-working, prudent man, careful of his earnings, and strictly honest who complained of bad luck.

Henry Ward Beecher

We should not judge people by their peak of excellence; but by the distance they have traveled from the point where they started.

Henry Ward Beecher

It is not the going out of port, but the coming in, that determines the success of a voyage.

Henry Ward Beecher

Every young man would do well to remember that all successful business stands on the foundation of morality.

Henry Ward Beecher

The meanest, most contemptible kind of praise is that which first speaks well of a man, and then qualifies it with a "but".

Henry Ward Beecher

The ability to convert ideas to things is the secret of outward success.

Henry Ward Beecher

To become an able and successful man in any profession, three things are necessary, nature, study and practice.

Henry Ward Beecher

Big results require big ambitions.

Heraclitus

No one that encounters prosperity does not also encounter danger.

Heraclitus

He who has never failed somewhere, that man can not be great.

Herman Melville

There are some enterprises in which a careful disorderliness is the true method.

Herman Melville

There is nothing namable but that some men will, or undertake to, do it for pay.

Herman Melville

There is all of the difference in the world between paying and being paid.

Herman Melville

Those who spend too fast never grow rich.

Honore de Balzac

Gentlemen, when the enemy is committed to a mistake we must not interrupt him too soon.

Horatio Nelson

First gain the victory and then make the best use of it you can.

Horatio Nelson

Desperate affairs require desperate measures.

Horatio Nelson

It is beyond a doubt that all our knowledge that begins with experience.

Immanuel Kant

To be is to do.

Immanuel Kant

Well-arranged time is the surest mark of a well-arranged mind.

Isaac Pitman

When you expect things to happen - strangely enough - they do happen.

J.P. Morgan

The practical effect of a belief is the real test of its soundness.

James Anthony Froude

If you review the commercial history, you will discover anyone who controls oriental trade will get hold of global wealth.

James J. Hill

The circulation of confidence is better than the circulation of money.

James Madison

A little flattery will support a man through great fatigue.

James Monroe

I do not say that, when brought to the test, I shall be invincible.

James Otis

Let the consequences be what they will, I am determined to proceed.

James Otis

We can recognize the dawn and the decline of love by the uneasiness we feel when alone together.

Jean de la Bruyere

A vain man finds it wise to speak good or ill of himself; a modest man does not talk of himself.

Jean de la Bruyere

It is a sad thing when men have neither the wit to speak well nor the judgment to hold their tongues.

Jean de la Bruyere

Out of difficulties grow miracles.

Jean de la Bruyere

The giving is the hardest part; what does it cost to add a smile?

Jean de la Bruyere

Those who make the worst use of their time are the first to complain of its brevity.

Jean de la Bruyere

Be great in act, as you have been in thought.

Jean Paul

You prove your worth with your actions, not with your mouth.

Jean Paul

When something an affliction happens to you, you either let it defeat you, or you defeat it.

Jean-Jacques Rousseau

Patience is bitter, but its fruit is sweet.

Jean-Jacques Rousseau

A man can do what he ought to do; and when he says he cannot, it is because he will not.

Johann Gottlieb Fichte

Who makes quick use of the moment is a genius of prudence.

Johann Kaspar Lavater

He who seldom speaks, and with one calm well-timed word can strike dumb the loquacious, is a genius or a hero.

Johann Kaspar Lavater

A good idea plus capable men cannot fail; it is better than money in the bank.

John Berry

The result showed the wisdom of your orders.

John Bigelow

The greatest ability in business is to get along with others and to influence their actions.

John Hancock

An executive is a person who always decides sometimes he decides correctly, but he always decides.

John Henry Patterson

To survive, men and business and corporations must serve.

John Henry Patterson

I have not yet begun to fight!

John Paul Jones

All good things which exist are the fruits of originality.

John Stuart Mill

One person with a belief is equal to a force of ninety-nine who have only interest.

John Stuart Mill

Any seeming deception in a statement is costly, not only in the expense of the advertising but in the detrimental effect produced upon the customer, who believes she has been misled.

John Wanamaker

Half the money I spend on advertising is wasted; the trouble is, I don't know which half.

John Wanamaker

Nothing comes merely by thinking about it.

John Wanamaker

When a customer enters my store, forget me. He is king.

John Wanamaker

I never knew a man come to greatness or eminence who lay abed late in the morning.

Jonathan Swift

There are few, very few, that will own themselves in a mistake.

Jonathan Swift

A selfish man is a thief.

Jose Marti

An insatiable appetite for glory leads to sacrifice and death, but innate instinct leads to self-preservation and life.

Jose Marti

Like stones rolling down hills, fair ideas reach their objectives despite all obstacles and barriers. It may be possible to speed or hinder them, but impossible to stop them.

Jose Marti

One is guilty of all abjection that one does not help to relieve.

Jose Marti

You cannot teach old dogs new tricks.

Joseph Chamberlain

A feeble executive implies a feeble execution of the government.

Joseph Story

Economy is a savings-bank, into which men drop pennies, and get dollars in return.

Josh Billings

One of rarest things that a man ever does is to do the best he can.

Josh Billings

I never could be good when I was not happy

Julia Ward Howe

Experience is the teacher of all things.

Julius Caesar

It is better to create than to learn! Creating is the essence of life.

Julius Caesar

Sell a man a fish, he eats for a day, teach a man how to fish, you ruin a wonderful business opportunity.

Karl Marx

It is even better to act quickly and err than to hesitate until the time of action is past.

Karl Clausewitz

To see things in the seed, that is genius.

Lao Tzu

The power of intuitive understanding will protect you from harm until the end of your days.

Lao Tzu

The journey of a thousand miles begins with one step.

Lao Tzu

Respond intelligently even to unintelligent treatment.

Lao Tzu

Mastering others is strength. Mastering yourself is true power.

Lao Tzu

An ant on the move does more than a dozing ox.

Lao Tzu

When the best leader's work is done the people say, "We did it ourselves."

Lao Tzu

To lead people walk behind them.

Lao Tzu

Silence is a source of great strength.

Lao Tzu

One who is too insistent on his own views, finds few to agree with him.

Lao Tzu

Nature does not hurry, yet everything is accomplished.

Lao Tzu

Great acts are made up of small deeds.

Lao Tzu

Give a man a fish and you feed him for a day. Teach him how to fish and you feed him for a lifetime.

Lao Tzu

Anticipate the difficult by managing the easy.

Lao Tzu

I take a simple view of life. It is keep your eyes open and get on with it.

Laurence Sterne

There is only one time that is important - NOW! It is the most important time because it is the only time that we have any power.

Leo Tolstoy

The great recipe for success is to work, and always work.

Leon Gambetta

People may doubt what you say, but they will believe what you do.

Lewis Cass

He who believes is strong; he who doubts is weak. Strong convictions precede great actions.

Louisa May Alcott

Belief in oneself is one of the most important bricks in building any successful venture.

Lydia Child

Give a man a fish and you feed him for a day; teach a man to fish and you feed him for a lifetime.

Maimonides

The risk of a wrong decision is preferable to the terror of indecision.

Maimonides

Tomorrow is nothing, today is too late; the good lived yesterday.

Marcus Aurelius

That which is not good for the bee-hive cannot be good for the bees.

Marcus Aurelius

The secret of all victory lies in the organization of the non-obvious.

Marcus Aurelius

You have power over your mind - not outside events. Realize this, and you will find strength.

Marcus Aurelius

Confine yourself to the present.

Marcus Aurelius

Don't organize for any other purpose than mutual benefit to the employer and the employee.

Mark Hanna

It is better to deserve honors and not have them than to have them and not deserve them.

Mark Twain

The dictionary is the only place where success comes before work.

Mark Twain

I was gratified to be able to answer promptly, and I did. I said I didn't know.

Mark Twain

A man with a surplus can control circumstances, but a man without a surplus is controlled by them, and often has no opportunity to exercise judgment.

Marshall Field

Good will is the one and only asset that competition cannot undersell or destroy

Marshall Field

Right or wrong, the customer is always right.

Marshall Field

The more business one has, the more you are able to accomplish, for you learn to economize your time.

Matthew Hale

Do exactly what you would do if you felt most secure.

Meister Eckhart

The price of inaction is far greater than the cost of making a mistake.

Meister Eckhart

Truth uttered before its time is always dangerous.

Mencius

He who establishes his argument by noise and command shows that his reason is weak.

Michel de Montaigne

I study myself more than any other subject. That is my metaphysics, that is my physics.

Michel de Montaigne

Not being able to govern events, I govern myself.

Michel de Montaigne

No wind serves him who addresses his voyage to no certain port.

Michel de Montaigne

In order to attain the impossible, one must attempt the absurd.

Miguel de Cervantes

One of the most considerable advantages the great have over their inferiors is to have servants as good as themselves.

Miguel de Cervantes

That which costs little is less valued.

Miguel de Cervantes

Perceive that which cannot be seen with the eye.

Miyamoto Musashi

Do nothing which is of no use.

Miyamoto Musashi

Perceive that which cannot be seen with the eye.

Miyamoto Musashi

Do nothing which is of no use.

Miyamoto Musashi

You win battles by knowing the enemy's timing, and using a timing which the enemy does not expect.

Miyamoto Musashi

Study strategy over the years and achieve the spirit of the warrior. Today is victory over yourself of yesterday; tomorrow is your victory over lesser men.

Miyamoto Musashi

You win battles by knowing the enemy's timing, and using a timing which the enemy does not expect.

Miyamoto Musashi

Study strategy over the years and achieve the spirit of the warrior. Today is victory over yourself of yesterday; tomorrow is your victory over lesser men.

Miyamoto Musashi

Ability is nothing without opportunity.

Napolean Bonaparte

Impossible is a word to be found only in the dictionary of fools.

Napolean Bonaparte

He who fears being conquered is sure of defeat.

Napolean Bonaparte

A leader is a dealer in hope.

Napolean Bonaparte

One must change one's tactics every ten years if one wishes to maintain one's superiority.

Napolean Bonaparte

Take time to deliberate, but when the time for action has arrived, stop thinking and go in.

Napolean Bonaparte

Victory belongs to the most persevering.

Napolean Bonaparte

Never interrupt your enemy when he is making a mistake.

Napolean Bonaparte

The truest wisdom is a resolute determination.

Napolean Bonaparte

The act of policing is, in order to punish less often, to punish more severely.

Napolean Bonaparte

You must not fight too often with one enemy, or you will teach him all your art of war.

Napolean Bonaparte

Forethought we may have, undoubtedly, but not foresight.

Napolean Bonaparte

I am sometimes a fox and sometimes a lion. The whole secret of government lies in knowing when to be the one or the other.

Napolean Bonaparte

I made all my generals out of mud.

Napolean Bonaparte

If you want a thing done well, do it yourself.

Napolean Bonaparte

When small men attempt great enterprises, they always end by reducing them to the level of their mediocrity.

Napolean Bonaparte

Get there first with the most.

Nathan Bedford Forrest

Never stand and take a charge... charge them too.

Nathan Bedford Forrest

We are like the mechanism of a watch: each part is essential.

Nathan Mayer Rothschild

Necessity has no law.

Oliver Cromwell

He who stops being better stops being good.

Oliver Cromwell

Not only strike while the iron is hot, but make it hot by striking.

Oliver Cromwell

A few honest men are better than numbers.

Oliver Cromwell

The whole point of getting things done is knowing what to leave undone.

Oswald Chambers

The main thing is to make history, not to write it.

Otto von Bismarck

Anybody can cut prices, but it takes brains to make a better article

Philip Armour

Either I will find a way, or I will make one.

Philip Sidney

The easiest way to be cheated is to believe yourself to be more cunning than others.

Pierre Charron

The beginning is the most important part of the work.

Plato

Hardly any human being is capable of pursuing two professions or two arts rightly

Plato

A good decision is based on knowledge and not on numbers.

Plato

There is no harm in repeating a good thing.

Plato

Wise men talk because they have something to say; fools, because they have to say something.

Plato

Rhetoric is the art of ruling the minds of men.

Plato

The measure of a man is what he does with power.

Plato

Never discourage anyone.....who continually makes progress, no matter how slow.

Plato

He is not wise to me who is wise in words only, but he who is wise in deeds.

Pope Gregory I

Man is the measure of all things, of things that are that they are, and of things that are not that they are not.

Protagoras

We are not interested in the possibilities of defeat. They do not exist.

Queen Victoria

Whilst we deliberate how to begin a thing, it grows too late to begin it.

Quintilian

We excuse our sloth under the pretext of difficulty.

Quintilian

Though ambition in itself is a vice, yet it is often the parent of virtues.

Quintilian

Build a better mousetrap and the world will beat a path to your door.

Ralph Waldo Emerson

What you do speaks so loud that I cannot hear what you say.

Ralph Waldo Emerson

An ounce of action is worth a ton of theory

Ralph Waldo Emerson

If you want to go east, don't go west.

Ramakrishna

Change is not made without inconvenience, even from worse to better.

Richard Hooker

A minute's success pays the failure of years.

Robert Browning

The critical ingredient is getting off your butt and doing something. It's as simple as that. A lot of people have ideas, but there are few who decide to do something about them now. Not tomorrow. Not next week. But today. The true entrepreneur is a doer, not a dreamer.

Robert Browning

I cannot trust a man to control others who cannot control himself.

Robert E. Lee

Effective management always means asking the right question.

Robert Heller

Never ignore a gut feeling, but never believe that it's enough.

Robert Heller

*The first myth of management is that it exists. The second myth of management
is that success equals skill.*

Robert Heller

Few rich men own their own property. The property owns them.

Robert Ingersoll

*The bold enterprises are the successful ones. Take counsel of hopes rather than of
fears to win in this business.*

Rutherford B. Hayes

The scars of others should teach us caution.

Saint Jerome

Be gentle to all and stern with yourself.

Saint Teresa of Avila

To reach something good it is very useful to have gone astray, and thus acquire experience.

Saint Teresa of Avila

Every man is the architect of his own fortune.

Sallust

We employ the mind to rule, the body to serve.

Sallust

We are what we repeatedly do. Excellence, then, is a habit.

Socrates

If a man is proud of his wealth, he should not be praised until it is known how he employs it.

Socrates

To dare is to lose one's footing momentarily. Not to dare is to lose oneself.

Soren Kierkegaard

Trouble is the common denominator of living. It is the great equalizer.

Soren Kierkegaard

During the first period of a man's life the greatest danger is not to take the risk.

Soren Kierkegaard

The tyrant dies and his rule is over, the martyr dies and his rule begins.

Soren Kierkegaard

Always mystify, mislead and surprise the enemy if possible.

Stonewall Jackson

The general who wins the battle makes many calculations in his temple before the battle is fought. The general who loses makes but few calculations beforehand.

Sun Tzu

Opportunities multiply as they are seized.

Sun Tzu

You have to believe in yourself.

Sun Tzu

Can you imagine what I would do if I could do all I can?

Sun Tzu

Thus, what is of supreme importance in war is to attack the enemy's strategy.

Sun Tzu

The supreme art of war is to subdue the enemy without fighting.

Sun Tzu

Pretend inferiority and encourage his arrogance.

Sun Tzu

Invincibility lies in the defense; the possibility of victory in the attack.

Sun Tzu

If you are far from the enemy, make him believe you are near.

Sun Tzu

He who knows when he can fight and when he cannot, will be victorious.

Sun Tzu

All warfare is based on deception.

Sun Tzu

The boy who is going to make a great man must not make up his mind merely to overcome a thousand obstacles, but to win in spite of a thousand repulses and defeats.

Theodore Roosevelt

It is only through labor and painful effort, by grim energy and resolute courage, that we move on to better things.

Theodore Roosevelt

The most important single ingredient in the formula of success is knowing how to get along with people.

Theodore Roosevelt

Far and away the best prize that life has to offer is the chance to work hard at work worth doing.

Theodore Roosevelt

Do what you can, with what you have, where you are.

Theodore Roosevelt

In a moment of decision the best thing you can do is the right thing. The worst thing you can do is nothing.

Theodore Roosevelt

The best executive is the one who has sense enough to pick good men to do what he wants done, and self-restraint to keep from meddling with them while they do it.

Theodore Roosevelt

Big jobs usually go to the men who prove their ability to outgrow small ones.

Theodore Roosevelt

People ask the difference between a leader and a boss. The leader works in the open, and the boss in covert. The leader leads, and the boss drives.

Theodore Roosevelt

When you are asked if you can do a job, tell 'em, "Certainly I can!" Then get busy and find out how to do it.

Theodore Roosevelt

Courtesy is as much a mark of a gentleman as courage.

Theodore Roosevelt

Time is the most valuable thing a man can spend.

Theophrastus

If the highest aim of a captain were to preserve his ship, he would keep it in port forever.

Thomas Aquinas

A single breaker may recede; but the tide is evidently coming in.

Thomas B. Macaulay

Nothing except the mint can make money without advertising.

Thomas B. Macaulay

The object of oratory alone in not truth, but persuasion.

Thomas B. Macaulay

A strong mind always hopes, and has always cause to hope.

Thomas Carlyle

Do the duty which lies nearest to you, the second duty will then become clearer.

Thomas Carlyle

A man without a goal is like a ship without a rudder.

Thomas Carlyle

A man lives by believing something: not by debating and arguing about many things.

Thomas Carlyle

Conviction is worthless unless it is converted into conduct.

Thomas Carlyle

I've got a great ambition to die of exhaustion rather than boredom.

Thomas Carlyle

No pressure, no diamonds.

Thomas Carlyle

Our main business is not to see what lies dimly at a distance,but to do what lies clearly at hand.

Thomas Carlyle

Silence is more eloquent than words.

Thomas Carlyle

The greatest of all faults, I should say, is to be conscious of none.

Thomas Carlyle

A person who is gifted sees the essential point and leaves the rest as surplus.

Thomas Carlyle

Every noble work is at first impossible.

Thomas Carlyle

Everywhere in life, the true question is not what we gain, but what we do.

Thomas Carlyle

He who could foresee affairs three days in advance would be rich for thousands of years.

Thomas Carlyle

Thought is the parent of the deed.

Thomas Carlyle

A wise man turns chance into good fortune.

Thomas Fuller

Always mystify, mislead and surprise the enemy if possible.

Thomas J. Jackson

When angry count to ten before you speak. If very angry, count to one hundred

Thomas Jefferson

Delay is preferable to error.

Thomas Jefferson

It takes time to persuade men to do even what is for their own good.

Thomas Jefferson

Never spend your money before you have earned it.

Thomas Jefferson

Nothing gives one person so much advantage over another as to remain always cool and unruffled under all circumstances.

Thomas Jefferson

Speeches that are measured by the hour will die with the hour.

Thomas Jefferson

The moment a person forms a theory, his imagination sees in every object only the tracts which favor that theory.

Thomas Jefferson

To waken interest and kindle enthusiasm is the sure way to teach easily and successfully.

Tyron Edwards

Right actions in the future are the best apologies for bad actions in the past.

Tyron Edwards

Between two evils, choose neither; between two goods, choose both.

Tyron Edwards

Labor disgraces no man, but occasionally men disgrace labor.

Ulysses S. Grant

The way to get started is to quit talking and begin doing.

Walt Disney

It's kind of fun to do the impossible.

Walt Disney

Do what you do so well that they will want to see it again and bring their friends

Walt Disney

All our dreams can come true, if we have the courage to pursue them.

Walt Disney

A person should set his goals as early as he can and devote all his energy and talent to getting there. With enough effort, he may achieve it. Or he may find something that is even more rewarding.

Walt Disney

If you can dream it, you can do it.

Walt Disney

A man should never neglect his family for business.

Walt Disney

You may not realize it when it happens, but a kick in the teeth may be the best thing in the world for you.

Walt Disney

Get a good idea and stay with it. Do it, and work at it until it's done right.

Walt Disney

Of all the things I have done, the most vital is coordinating the talents of those who work for us and pointing them towards a certain goal.

Walt Disney

For success, attitude is equally as important as ability.

Walter Scott

Of all vices, drinking is the most incompatible with greatness.

Walter Scott

Success - keeping your mind awake and your desire asleep.

Walter Scott

Little minds are tamed and subdued by misfortune; but great minds rise above them.

Washington Irving

There is never jealousy where there is not strong regard

Washington Irving

The easiest thing to do, whenever you fail, is to put yourself down by blaming your lack of ability for your misfortunes.

Washington Irving

Men become wise just as they become rich, more by what they save than by what they receive.

Wilbur Wright

We must wake ourselves up! Or somebody else will take our place, and bear our cross, and thereby rob us of our crown.

William Booth

The sea hath fish for every man.

William Camden

You never know what you can do till you try.

William Cobbett

The one thing you can't do when you're highly ranked is relax.

William Floyd

I believe that economists put decimal points in their forecasts to show they have a sense of humor.

William Gilmore Simms

No man ever became great or good except through many and great mistakes.

William Gladstone

A chain is no stronger than its weakest link, and life is after all a chain.

William James

Action may not bring happiness but there is no happiness without action.

William James

If you want a quality, act as if you already had it.

William James

Most people never run far enough on their first wind to find out they've got a second.

William James

I will act as if what I do makes a difference.

William James

It is our attitude at the beginning of a difficult task which, more than anything else, will affect its successful outcome.

William James

Pessimism leads to weakness, optimism to power.

William James

To study the abnormal is the best way of understanding the normal.

William James

In the time of darkest defeat, victory may be nearest.

William McKinley

Expositions are the timekeepers of progress.

William McKinley

Rarely promise, but, if lawful, constantly perform.

William Penn

Time is what we want most, but what we use worst.

William Penn

No man pays double or twice for the same thing, forasmuch as nothing can be spent but once.

William Petty

We are what we repeatedly do. Excellence, then, is not an act, it is a habit.

William Prescott

Curiosity is, in great and generous minds, the first passion and the last.

William Samuel Johnson

Our doubts are traitors, and make us lose the good we oft might win by fearing to attempt.

William Shakespeare

People don't follow titles, they follow courage.

William Wells Brown

Every failure is a step to success.

William Whewell

The sweetest of all sounds is praise.

Xenophon

The person attempting to travel two roads at once will get nowhere.

Xun Zi